Wonders Built by Humans

THE GOLDEN GATE BRIDGE

Sloane Gould

CREATED BY Humans

Published in 2026 by The Rosen Publishing Group, Inc.
2544 Clinton Street, Buffalo, NY 14224

First Edition

Editor: Caitie McAneney
Designer: Rachel Rising

Photo Credits: Cover, Philippe M Newman/Shutterstock.com; Cover, (series background) Yuliya Chsherbakova/Shutterstock.com; p. 5 Sergii Figurnyi/Shutterstock.com; p. 7 Rudy Balasko/Shutterstock.com; p. 9 https://commons.wikimedia.org/wiki/File:Entrance_to_Golden_Gate_and_Angel_Island_(before_the_bridge),_San_Francisco,_ca.1900_(CHS-3943A).jpg; p.11 Christopher Penler/Shutterstock.com; p. 13 Fast Speeds Imagery/ Shutterstock.com; p. 13 VolareVideo/Shutterstock.com; p. 14 Cinar12345/Shutterstock.com; p. 15 https://commons.wikimedia.org/wiki/File:Construction_of_the_Golden_Gate_Bridge_3c22793u.jpg; p. 17 https://commons.wikimedia.org/wiki/File:Photograph_of_the_Golden_Gate_Bridge_under_construction.jpg; p. 18 DTM Media/Shutterstock.com; p. 19 Fast Speeds Imagery/Shutterstock.com; p. 21 Oomka/Shutterstock.com; p. 23 Alexander Demyanenko/Shutterstock.com; p. 24 beeboys/Shutterstock.com; p. 25 Sean Pavone/Shutterstock.com; p. 27 gob_cu/Shutterstock.com; p. 29 FERNANDO BLANCO CALZADA/Shutterstock.com.

Cataloging-in-Publication Data

Names: Gould, Sloane.
Title: The Golden Gate Bridge / Sloane Gould.
Description: Buffalo, NY : Created by Humans, an imprint of Rosen Publishing, 2026. | Series: Wonders built by humans | Includes glossary and index.
Identifiers: ISBN 9781534552937 (pbk.) | ISBN 9781534552944 (library bound) | ISBN 9781534552951 (ebook)
Subjects: LCSH: Golden Gate Bridge (San Francisco, Calif.)--Juvenile literature.
Classification: LCC TG25.S225 G685 2026 | DDC 624.230979461--dc23

Manufactured in China

CPSIA Compliance Information: Batch #QWCBH26. For Further Information contact Rosen Publishing at 1-800-237-9932.

CONTENTS

A BOLD BRIDGE

Bridges are some of the most amazing structures built by humans. They are valuable links between places, and allow for important movement of goods and people. Bridges are built over rivers, valleys, and canyons. There are many different designs, from arches to suspension bridges. Some of them are small. Others are miles long!

The Golden Gate Bridge is a true wonder of engineering. When it opened in 1937, it was the longest suspension bridge in the world. It took human creativity and **ingenuity** to overcome the challenges of building this bridge. It is a **symbol** of its home city of San Francisco, California, and one of the most famous bridges in the world!

WOW!

The Golden Gate Bridge is 1.7 miles (2.7 km) long between the **abutments** on each end.

People can walk, bike, or drive across the Golden Gate Bridge.

WORLD'S LONGEST!

Humans have created bridges for thousands of years. As **technology** advanced, they had stronger materials and new ideas for designs. The Golden Gate Bridge built on the ideas that had been developed over centuries.

Before the Golden Gate Bridge was built, the longest bridge in the world was the George Washington Bridge. This suspension bridge crosses the Hudson River from New Jersey to Manhattan in New York City. It opened in 1931. When the Golden Gate Bridge opened just six years later, it was much longer!

WOW!

The original span of the George Washington Bridge was 3,500 feet (1,067 m).

When it was built, the George Washington Bridge was double the size of the longest suspension bridge in the world.

A GREAT CHALLENGE

The Golden Gate Bridge connects the city of San Francisco to Marin County. This is the city's neighbor to the north, but they were separated by the Golden Gate. This **strait** lies between the Pacific Ocean and San Francisco Bay. For a bridge to be built, it would have to span nearly a mile.

Some people called this bridge "the bridge that couldn't be built." Many politicians were against building it. Also, the **Great Depression** had stripped funds for public projects. Earthquakes, fog, and strong winds and tides were also challenges. It would take a genius to tackle the problem!

WOW!

Between the mid-1800s and 1900, San Francisco's population boomed because of a **gold rush**.

This photograph shows the Golden Gate before the bridge. Many Californians voted in favor of paying for a bridge to cross the strait.

AN ENGINEER AND A DREAMER

The man for the job was Joseph Strauss. When he was a young man at the University of Cincinnati, he was hurt while trying out for the football team. As he rested in the school's **infirmary**, he spotted the Cincinnati-Covington bridge from the window. It was the first long-span suspension bridge in the country. He was inspired!

Strauss worked as a draftsman for several years before becoming an engineer. He came up with a special drawbridge design. He made around 400 drawbridges in the United States. Then, he was asked about the "impossible" task of building a bridge over the Golden Gate. It excited him.

WOW!

As a draftsman, Strauss drew sketches and plans for structures to be built.

This statue of Joseph Strauss stands near the Golden Gate Bridge.

Joseph Strauss, the Poet

Joseph Strauss was born in Cincinnati, Ohio, in 1870. His whole family loved art, and he thought he might go into the arts as well. He loved poetry, and his classmates at the University of Cincinnati voted for him to be the class poet and class president. He wrote a poem when the Golden Gate Bridge was finished that read, "At last, the mighty task is done." He died soon after.

A DARING DESIGN

Strauss had built many drawbridges, but for this project, he realized a suspension bridge was the way to go. Suspension bridges rely on steel cables to hold up a roadway as it hangs in midair.

Strauss's design called for towers 746 feet (227 m) tall with thick cables holding up the bridge. The towers would have to be planted firmly in the rock beneath the water. The roadway would be held up by smaller cables as well. As for how the bridge would look, that job went to architect Irving Morrow, who chose an Art Deco look. This style uses bold shapes and colors.

WOW!

Engineers Charles Ellis and Leon Moissieff also **contributed** greatly to the Golden Gate's design. Moissieff was a suspension bridge expert.

Coming up with the plans for the Golden Gate Bridge was truly a team effort.

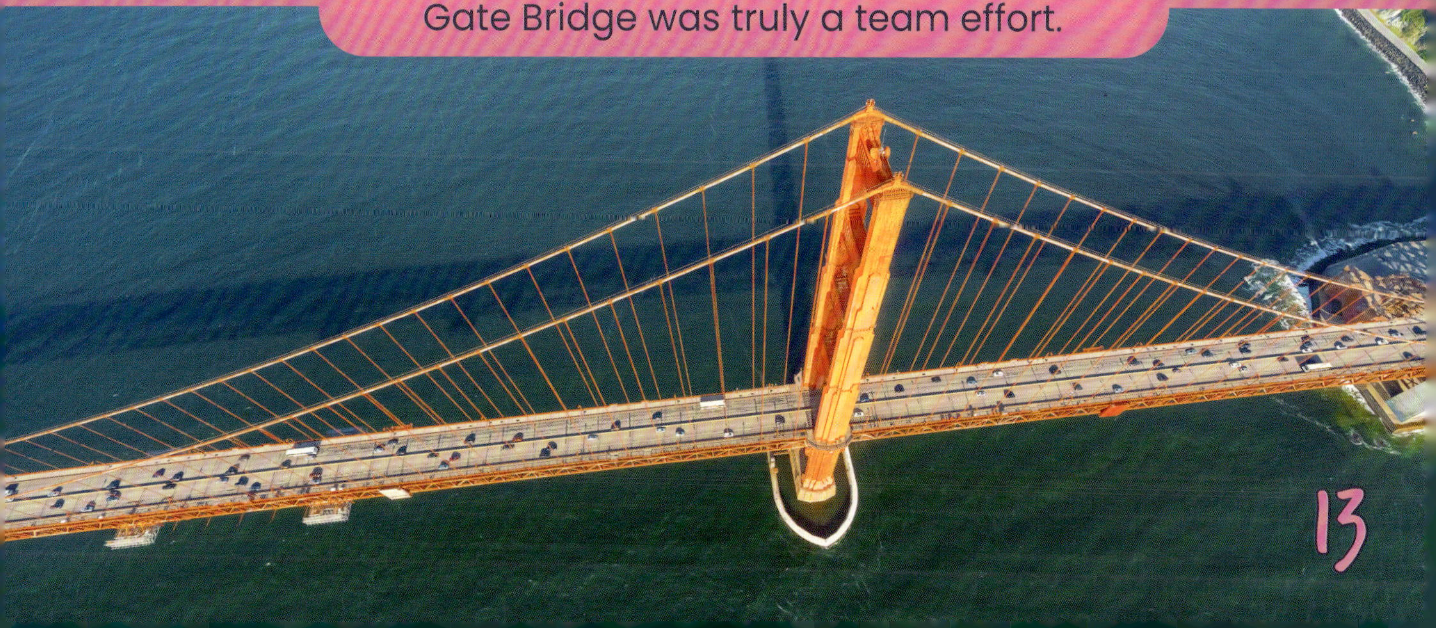

EARTHQUAKE-PROOF

San Francisco is no stranger to earthquakes. These ground-shaking events happen relatively often there. That's because the city sits near the San Andreas fault line. This is a place where two tectonic plates, or giant slabs of earth, meet. When they move, it causes the ground to shake. This can cause great harm to structures. The 1906 San Francisco Earthquake ruined nearly 80 percent of the city's structures!

Because of this, the design of the Golden Gate Bridge would have to keep earthquakes in mind. The towers would need to be secured in the rock underneath the deep water to be earthquake-proof.

Workers had to blast through the bedrock underneath the strait to secure the towers.

Ring of Fire

San Francisco is located on the Pacific Ring of Fire. That's a 25,000-mile (40,000 km) horseshoe-shaped area around the Pacific Ocean where there are many volcanoes and earthquakes due to shifting tectonic plates. The San Andreas Faultline is a part of this ring. It's about 800 miles (1,287.5 km) long, and it's between the Pacific and North American plates. Around 90 percent of all the earthquakes on Earth happen in the Ring of Fire.

BUILDING THE BRIDGE

Building the bridge was a test of human strength and **perseverance**. Many construction workers jumped at the chance to work on the bridge. That's because it was built during the Great Depression. In this time, 25 percent of Americans were out of work. Families went hungry. This bridge was an opportunity for many Americans.

One of the hardest jobs was building underwater. Divers went 110 feet (30.5 m) under water to put dynamite into the bedrock. Then, they placed concrete and pieces of the tower deep in the rock. Other workers had to climb hundreds of feet up the towers to secure the cables. It was very dangerous work.

Working high up meant dealing with wind, rain, fog, and very slippery conditions.

A Risky Job

A job working on the Golden Gate Bridge was risky. In fact, it could be deadly. People sometimes fell from great heights into the water. A total of 11 people died working on the bridge. A safety net was installed to catch people who fell. Ten men died when a scaffold broke and fell through the net. Divers had their own risks—they had to battle strong currents and relied on their oxygen tanks working.

INTERNATIONAL ORANGE

Apart from its size, one thing that sets the Golden Gate Bridge apart is its color. The color was chosen for how it looks as well as how it **functions**. While you may think the bridge would be gold, as its name suggests, it is actually a red-orange color. It's called "International Orange."

Architect Irving Morrow chose this color because it set the bridge apart from the ocean and sky. This is important on a foggy day when it's hard to see! It also blended nicely with the colors of the nearby hills. The color makes it a clear landmark in San Francisco!

The bridge is made of steel, which is usually a silver color. International Orange sets it apart!

A GRAND OPENING

After four years of hard work, the Golden Gate Bridge finally opened to **pedestrians** on May 27, 1937. Around 200,000 people walked across the bridge. It was 25 cents to try it out! This day kicked off a weeklong celebration that involved parades and parties. It was called the "Golden Gate Bridge Fiesta."

The next day, vehicles were allowed to cross the bridge. The president—Franklin Delano Roosevelt—announced the groundbreaking event via telegraph. It was a grand opening for a grand project! In just the first year, nearly 3.9 million vehicles and 400,000 pedestrians crossed the bridge.

When the Golden Gate Bridge opened, it was a treat to cross it. Now it's part of everyday life for people in San Francisco!

MAKING THE CONNECTION

The Golden Gate Bridge became an important link between San Francisco and its neighbors to the north. Before the bridge was built, people would have to take a ferryboat from the city to Marin County. This made it difficult to transport things or find work between the two places. It was also sometimes tricky to cross the strait by boat during bad weather or fog.

Connecting San Francisco and Marin County boosted tourism. People came to see the bridge itself. They also crossed the bridge from San Francisco to visit the natural areas in the north, including incredible redwood trees.

Work on the Golden Gate Bridge made way for the construction of nearby San Francisco-Oakland Bay Bridge, which connects Oakland, Yerba Buena Island, and San Francisco.

BREAKING RECORDS

The main span of the Golden Gate Bridge is 4,200 feet (1,280 m), which is about 0.8 mile (1.3 km). That broke records when it opened in 1937! It kept the record for the world's longest suspension bridge until 1964. The Verrazano-Narrows Bridge in New York took the lead that year. The Golden Gate is still the second-longest suspension bridge in the United States!

The Golden Gate Bridge inspired people around the world to make longer and longer bridges. The longest suspension bridge in the world today is the Akashi Kaikyo Bridge in Japan. It is 12,831 feet (3,911 m) long and made of three spans.

The Akashi Kaikyo Bridge opened in 1998.

THE GOLDEN GATE BRIDGE TODAY

The American Society of Civil Engineers honored the Golden Gate Bridge as one of the "Seven Wonders of the United States" in 1994. It was due to the ingenuity of Joseph Strauss and the other engineers, architects, and workers who tackled the project. The team finished the bridge in less time and for less money than expected. They did the impossible.

Today, the Golden Gate Bridge sees 112,000 vehicles per day. There are also bicyclists zooming down the lanes on either side of them. Pedestrians walk the bridge to get a wonderful view of San Francisco. The bridge is truly a wonder!

The Golden Gate Bridge is part of Highway 101, which stretches from Los Angeles, California, to Olympia, Washington.

YOU CAN DESIGN IT!

Imagine you must design a bridge in your community or city. It needs to be strong enough to withstand earthquakes and poor weather. It needs to be designed with safety in mind for pedestrians and drivers.

Ask yourself:

- Where would I put my bridge?
- What materials will I use?
- Would I use an arch or suspension design?
- How can I make it stand for centuries?

Sketch out some plans for your bridge on a separate sheet of paper.

Bonus: Share your ideas with friends, or build a **prototype** out of found materials!

Designing bridges uses every part of STEM—science, technology, engineering, and math!

GLOSSARY

abutment: Something against which another thing rests its weight or pushes with force.
contribute: To give along with others.
function: Something for which a person or thing is specially fitted or used.
gold rush: A rush to newly discovered goldfields in pursuit of riches.
Great Depression: The period of severe worldwide economic decline that began in 1929 and lasted throughout the 1930s and that was marked by deflation and widespread unemployment.
infirmary: A place in a school where people receive care for an illness or injury.
ingenuity: Skill or cleverness that allows people to solve problems and create inventions.
pedestrian: A person going on foot.
perseverance: The state of continuing on with something even in the face of challenges.
prototype: An original model on which something is patterned.
strait: A narrow passageway connecting two large bodies of water.
symbol: Something that stands for something else.
technology: Using science, engineering, and other industries to invent useful tools or to solve problems. Also a machine, piece of equipment, or method created by technology.

FOR MORE INFORMATION

BOOKS

Kelley, Tera. *Golden Gate Bridge.* Mendota Heights, MN: Apex Editions, 2024.

Luciow, Chelsey. *Build 10 Bold Bridges with STEM*. North Mankato, MN: Capstone Press, 2025.

McAneney, Caitie. *20 Fun Facts About Famous Bridges*. New York, NY: Gareth Stevens Publishing, 2020.

WEBSITES

Golden Gate Bridge
kids.britannica.com/kids/article/Golden-Gate-Bridge/601414
Read more facts about the Golden Gate Bridge with Britannica Kids!

Golden Gate Bridge Chronology
www.pbs.org/wgbh/americanexperience/features/goldengate-timeline
Check out a timeline of the building of the Golden Gate Bridge.

Joseph Strauss
www.pbs.org/wgbh/americanexperience/features/goldengate-strauss
Learn more about the creative mind behind the Golden Gate Bridge, Joseph Strauss.

INDEX